KING TUT

Natalie Hyde

CRABTREE
Publishing Company
www.crabtreebooks.com

Crabtree Publishing Company
www.crabtreebooks.com

Author: Natalie Hyde
**Publishing plan research
and development:** Reagan Miller
Editors: Sonya Newland, Kathy Middleton
Proofreader: Shannon Welbourn
Photo Researcher: Sonya Newland
Design: Tim Mayer
Cover design: Ken Wright
Illustrator: Stefan Chabluk
**Production coordinator and
prepress tecnician:** Ken Wright
Print coordinator: Margaret Amy Salter

Produced for Crabtree Publishing
Company by White-Thomson Publishing

Photographs:
Alamy: Danita Delimont: p. 41; Corbis:
Sandro Vannini: pp. 11, 34; Stefano Bianchetti:
pp. 16–17; National Geographic Society:
pp. 20–21; PoodlesRock: p. 40; Ben Curtis/
pool/epa: p. 42; Taylor S. Kennedy/National
Geographic Society: pp. 44–45; Dreamstime:
Haak78: p. 38; Prehor: p. 39; Getty Images:
pp. 5, 28–29, 32–33; Hisham Ibrahim: p. 4;
UIG: pp. 10–11, 27; De Agostini: pp. 30-31;
Kenneth Garrett: pp. 36–37; Shutterstock:
Mirek Hejnicki: pp. 6–7; WitR: pp. 8–9,
12–13; Ilia Torlin: p. 18; BasPhoto: pp. 18–19;
Federico Rostagno: p. 22; Rachelle Burnside:
p. 23; Vladimir Wrange: p. 25; ostill: p. 43;
SuperStock: Robert Harding Picture Library:
pp. 14–15, 35; Science and Society: p. 24;
David Cole/age footstock: p. 26; © Leemage/
The Bridgeman Art Library: front cover.

Library and Archives Canada Cataloguing in Publication

Hyde, Natalie, 1963-, author
    King Tut / Natalie Hyde.

(Crabtree chrome)
Includes index.
Issued in print and electronic formats.
ISBN 978-0-7787-1172-8 (bound).--ISBN 978-0-7787-1181-0 (pbk.).--
ISBN 978-1-4271-8933-2 (pdf).--ISBN 978-1-4271-8925-7 (html)

    1. Tutankhamen, King of Egypt--Tomb--Juvenile literature.
2. Egypt--Civilization--To 332 B.C.--Juvenile literature. I. Title.
II. Series: Crabtree chrome

DT87.5.H93 2013   j932'.014092   C2013-906224-6
                                           C2013-906225-4

Library of Congress Cataloging-in-Publication Data

Hyde, Natalie, 1963-
    King Tut / Natalie Hyde.
        pages cm. -- (Crabtree chrome)
    Includes index.
    ISBN 978-0-7787-1172-8 (reinforced library binding) --
ISBN 978-0-7787-1181-0 (pbk.) -- ISBN 978-1-4271-8933-2
(electronic pdf) -- ISBN 978-1-4271-8925-7 (electronic html)
    1. Tutankhamen, King of Egypt--Juvenile literature.
2. Tutankhamen, King of Egypt--Tomb--Juvenile literature.
3. Pharaohs--Biography--Juvenile literature. 4. Egypt--
History--Eighteenth dynasty, ca. 1570-1320 B.C.--Juvenile
literature. I. Title.

DT87.5.H94 2014
932'.014092--dc23
[B]
                                                   2013036062

Crabtree Publishing Company

www.crabtreebooks.com   1-800-387-7650

Printed in Canada/102013/BF20130920

Published in Canada
Crabtree Publishing
616 Welland Ave.
St. Catharines, ON
L2M 5V6

Published in the United States
Crabtree Publishing
PMB 59051
350 Fifth Avenue, 59th Floor
New York, New York 10118

Published in the United Kingdom
Crabtree Publishing
Maritime House
Basin Road North, Hove
BN41 1WR

Published in Australia
Crabtree Publishing
3 Charles Street
Coburg North
VIC 3058

Contents

The Lost King   4

Who Was the Boy Pharaoh?   8

Kings of Egypt   14

Finding Tut's Tomb   24

Tut's Treasures   30

Revealing Tut's Secrets   40

Learning More   46

Glossary   47

Index   48

The Lost King

▲ *Among the many beautiful treasures in Tut's tomb was a golden throne. On the back was a picture of the pharaoh and his wife.*

A Wonderful Discovery

Lord Carnarvon hurried to Egypt from England. He carried with him a telegram from the **archaeologist** Howard Carter. It read: "At last have made wonderful discovery in Valley; a magnificent tomb with seals intact." Years of searching had finally paid off. They had discovered the tomb of the ancient Egyptian king Tutankhamun.

◀ *Carter and his assistants peer into Tut's tomb. They were amazed by the riches that they found there.*

Breaking through

After days of digging through piles of stone rubble, they found a sealed door. Carter broke a hole in the plaster and peeked inside. What he saw by the light of his candle made him gasp. "Can you see anything?" Carnarvon asked. Carter replied: "Yes, wonderful things!"

Tutankhamun's tomb was the most complete tomb ever found in Egypt. Its discovery changed our knowledge and understanding of ancient Egypt. It also modernized methods of recording and preserving artifacts, which are objects made by humans.

archaeologist: someone who studies ancient people

An Interest in Egypt

Lord Carnarvon was an **amateur** Egyptologist from England. An Egyptologist is someone who studies the history and culture of ancient Egypt. In 1914, Lord Carnarvon got permission from the Egyptian government to dig in the Valley of the Kings. Many of Egypt's pharaohs, or kings, were buried there. Some archaeologists believed that all the tombs had been found. Lord Carnarvon thought they were wrong.

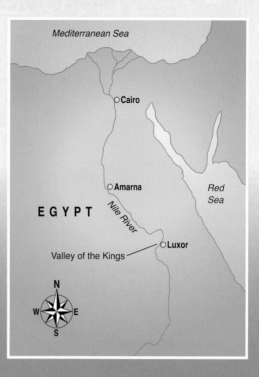

▲ *This map shows some of the main sites in Egypt, including the Valley of the Kings, where Tut's tomb was found.*

The Search for Tutankhamun

Carnarvon hired British archaeologist Howard Carter to look for new tombs. In earlier explorations, Carter had found clues that a pharaoh named Tutankhamun was buried in the valley. The young archaeologist was sure Tut's tomb was still hidden underground. But, by 1922, Lord Carnarvon was running out of money. He could only afford to pay the workers for one more season. Then Carter made his amazing discovery.

▼ *Today, we know that there are more than 60 royal tombs in the Valley of the Kings, near Luxor in Egypt.*

Lord Carnarvon (1866–1923) was a rich English earl. He owned racehorses and later became interested in ancient Egypt. Archaeologist Howard Carter (1874–1939) was only 17 when he first went to Egypt. He developed a more effective way of searching for tombs, by dividing the land into grids.

 amateur: someone who does something as a hobby not a job

Who Was the Boy Pharaoh?

Egypt's Great Houses

Ancient Egypt was ruled by pharaohs. A pharaoh was the political and religious leader of the land. The word "pharaoh" means "great house," which refers to the palaces where they lived. Both men and women could become pharaoh, but power was usually passed from father to son.

Becoming Pharaoh

Tutankhamun's father, Akhenaten, died when Tut was young. His elder brother had also died. This meant that Tut was next in line to inherit the throne. He became pharaoh when he was only nine years old, in about 1332 BCE. Trusted **advisors** helped him rule Egypt while he was still a child.

◀ *The ruins of great palaces and temples built to honor the pharaohs can still be seen in Egypt.*

Akhenaten made big changes to Egypt's religion during his time as pharaoh. Before his reign, Egyptians worshiped many gods. Akhenaten ordered that they should worship only one god—Aten, the Sun god. After Akhenaten's death, angry priests destroyed all traces of his name, and Egyptians went back to worshiping many gods.

advisors: experts who give advice to a leader

A Royal Childhood

Tutankhamun grew up in the royal palace in the capital city of Amarna. As the son of a pharaoh, he had the best food and wore the finest linen clothes. He was cared for by nannies and educated in the "kap," or royal nursery.

▼ *Little remains today of the palace at Amarna where Tutankhamun spent his childhood. This is part of the garden.*

An Egyptian Education

The young prince received the best education. He was taught reading, writing, and mathematics. He spent many hours learning picture writing called hieroglyphics. He would make hieroglyphs on **papyrus** using a reed brush and ink. His ink palette was made of ivory and his name was carved into it.

The hieroglyphs of royal names were always shown inside an oval ring called a cartouche. The ring symbolized eternal life. It was also believed to protect the name written inside.

◀ *This is Tutankhamun's cartouche. The three shapes at the top make up the word "Amun." In the middle, the bird and the two loaves of bread represent "Tut." On the left is the symbol for "Ankh," which means life.*

papyrus: a type of paper made from the stems of reed plants

Leisure Time

Life was not all about studying for the young Tutankhamun. On the hottest days, he went swimming in the nearby Nile River with his **siblings** and the children of other noble families. Nurses and guards stood on the shore, watching for dangerous crocodiles.

▶ *The Nile is the longest river in the world. It gave the ancient Egyptians water for drinking, washing, transportation, and growing crops.*

Out Hunting

One of Tutankhamun's favorite pastimes was hunting ducks. A miniature bow, made to fit a child's shorter arms, was found in his tomb. Images in his tomb show him hiding in the reeds, stalking his prey. His sisters helped by passing him arrows.

Around the age of eight, Tutankhamun was taught to drive a chariot, which was a two-wheeled cart pulled by horses. His teacher would help him practice for weeks to control two lively horses over uneven ground.

siblings: brothers and sisters

Kings of Egypt

The Power of the Pharaoh

To Egyptians, the pharaoh was more than a king. They believed their ruler was also a god. As well as running the country, the pharaoh had to keep the other gods happy with offerings and festivals. If he angered the gods, he could lose all his power. The pharaoh's main responsibility was to keep harmony, called Maat, within the country.

Egypt at War

Sometimes keeping Maat meant going to war to protect Egypt's borders. Tutankhamun fought with the Nubian people who lived in the south. But mainly he tried to keep good relations with neighboring peoples. After a battle, the defeated country would pay a **tribute** of valuable items like gems or gold to the pharaoh.

▼ *Paintings in Tut's tomb show him in his war chariot with his bow and arrow, fighting the enemy.*

As living gods, pharaohs were so important they did not even have to clean or dress themselves. That was the job of servants. One servant's job title was "Chief of the Scented Oils and Pastes for Rubbing His Majesty's Body."

tribute: a gift made to show respect

Preparing for Death

The ancient Egyptians believed in an **afterlife**. Pharaohs spent most of their lives preparing for death. As soon as a pharaoh was crowned, work would begin on the ruler's tomb. The first pharaohs had small tombs in the ground covered by a brick building, called a *mastaba*.

▼ *It may have taken 3,000–4,000 workers up to 30 years to build a pyramid for a pharaoh.*

Pyramid Tombs

Eventually, the *mastabas* became pyramids. Pyramids took thousands of workers many years to build. They were huge stone or brick structures, which could be seen from many miles away. This made them a target for tomb robbers, who wanted the precious objects that were buried with the pharaohs.

Tombs were built with hidden passages, trapdoors, or deep wells to confuse thieves. But this did not stop them. Often tombs were robbed by the men who built them. Some families were known as professional tomb robbers!

afterlife: life after death

Secret Graves

Later, pharaohs began looking for burial places that were more secret than pyramids to protect their tombs from robbers. The perfect place was discovered in a desert valley far from the Egyptian capital. Workers cut tombs deep into the **canyon** walls near the city of Luxor. They hoped this would make it harder for tomb robbers to find.

▼ *Once the tomb was dug out, artists and craftsmen would cover the walls with colorful paintings and beautiful carvings.*

The Valley of the Kings

This canyon is known today as the Valley of the Kings. The workers who built the tombs there lived in the nearby village of Deir el-Medina. A team of between 30 and 60 workers would dig, plaster, and paint a tomb in preparation for the pharaoh's death. Other important Egyptian men and women were also buried in the valley.

▼ *The village of Deir el-Medina, with about 60 houses, was home to the people who worked in the Valley of the Kings.*

Tutankhamun's tomb was raided twice before archaeologists discovered it in the 1900s. They found clues that made them think the robbers did not manage to steal much before they were caught. After each robbery, the tomb was resealed.

canyon: a deep valley with steep sides

Burial Rites

Tombs were built to hold all of the things the pharaoh would need in the afterlife, including his body. The walls and ceilings were decorated with scenes showing the gods helping the ruler on his journey after death. **Rituals** and prayers were also written on the walls. These were there to help the pharaoh move from death to his new life.

▼ *A funeral procession to a tomb cut into the rock. The boxes contain jewelry and other items that the Egyptians believed a person needed in the afterlife.*

Packing for the Afterlife

In the tombs were all the things people thought the dead would need in the afterlife. Pharaohs were used to a life of luxury. They were buried with piles of valuable jewelry, furniture, and weapons. They also stored food, drink, and clothing for their new life.

"It was as if they were packing for a trip to a place they had never visited and weren't sure what to bring, so they brought everything."

Egyptologist Bob Brier

 rituals: special ceremonies to mark particular events

21

Making Mummies

Egyptians believed that they needed their body in the afterlife, too. A mummy is a **preserved** body. The first bodies were mummified naturally in the dry sand of Egypt's deserts. Later, Egyptian priests learned how to use salt and chemicals to preserve bodies on purpose.

▼ *The bodies of the dead were carefully preserved with chemicals and wrapped in bandages.*

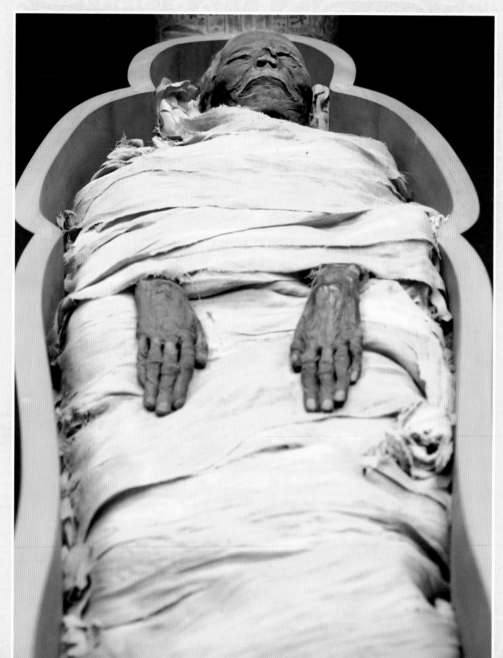

During mummification, the heart was left inside the body. The Egyptians believed the heart contained the soul. Using a hook inserted up the nose, the brain was removed and thrown away.

Organ Removal

First, the priests removed important organs from the body. They put the stomach, liver, lungs, and intestines in special containers, called canopic jars. The lids were decorated with the heads of gods. Afterward, the dried body was wrapped in linen strips and placed in a coffin.

◀ Canopic jars were made from limestone or clay. Each one held a particular organ such as the liver or lungs.

 preserved: kept in its original condition

Finding Tut's Tomb

A Sudden Death

Tutankhamun was still only a teenager when he died in about 1323 BCE. His tomb was not yet ready for him. The priests needed to find somewhere that could be completed quickly. They chose a smaller tomb that was being built for a nobleman. After the young pharaoh was buried, the entrance was covered with **rubble** from a nearby tomb.

▲ *It was hard to find the ancient tombs in the Valley of the Kings. Most of them had been covered with rock and sand for centuries.*

The Forgotten King

King Tut reigned only for a short time. There were few records left in Egypt of his life and deeds. Because his reign was unremarkable and his tomb was small for a pharaoh, people soon forgot the boy king's grave. While other tombs in the area were stripped of their precious objects, Tutankhamun's lack of fame protected his.

▲ *Today, the entrance to Tut's tomb is marked with a simple plaque with his name and the tomb number—62.*

The largest tomb in the Valley of the Kings is KV5. It was built for the sons of one of the greatest Egyptian pharaohs—Ramses II. Still being explored today, 121 passageways and rooms have been found so far, but there may be many more.

 rubble: pieces of stone left over from a building

Carter's Big Find

Thousands of years later, Howard Carter and his team stumbled across Tut's tomb in the Valley of the Kings. They found the steps under the ruins of a worker's house. This discovery sent a wave of excitement around the world. The doorways were still sealed—perhaps some treasures survived in the darkness of this tomb!

▼ *Howard Carter (on the left, standing on the steps) uses a metal bar to force open a room in Tutankhamun's tomb.*

A Treasure House

Not even Carter and Carnarvon could have imagined the riches that actually lay behind those doors. Tut's tomb turned out to be the most **intact** Egyptian burial place ever found. Inside, items were piled from floor to ceiling in four rooms. There was hardly space for the archaeologists to squeeze in to work.

Le Petit Journal *illustré*

Dans la poussière des Tombeaux

En Égypte, dans la Vallée des Rois, un archéologue anglais découvre une nouvelle sépulture. C'est, dans un état de conservation parfaite et remplie encore des objets précieux qu'on y avait déposés, la tombe du pharaon Tut-ankh-Amen, endormi depuis trois mille cinq cents ans.

▶ *The discovery was a sensation. Newspapers and magazines around the world told of the amazing treasures in Tut's tomb.*

Only a small portion of Tutankhamun's treasure has been displayed around the world. But the value of even that small portion is about three-quarters of a billion dollars!

intact: not broken or touched in any way

The Big Question

It was more than three months before Carter and Carnarvon were able to move enough objects to get to the burial room. The biggest question had still not been answered: was the mummy of Tutankhamun still inside? Or had it been moved or destroyed during the early robberies?

The Body of the King

When they finally reached the burial chamber, they found it was almost completely filled by four golden shrines stacked inside each other. Shrines are boxes that hold sacred items. Beneath the shrines was a **sarcophagus** that held three coffins, also one inside the other. The last coffin was made of solid gold. Incredibly, the mummy of King Tut was still inside!

◀ *No one could believe it when the last gold sarcophagus was opened, revealing the body of the boy king.*

Tutankhamun's now-famous death mask was placed on the head of the mummy. It is made of solid gold and was used to help the pharaoh's spirit recognize its body in the afterlife.

sarcophagus: a large stone coffin with smaller coffins inside

Tut's Treasures

A Pharaoh's Life in Artifacts

The many items in Tutankhamun's tomb revealed an enormous amount about the life of the pharaohs in ancient Egypt. There were so many things crammed into the four small rooms that it took Carter ten years to remove and catalog them all. In total, archaeologists found more than 5,000 objects.

Cataloging

Every item was numbered, described on a card, and photographed before it was removed from the tomb. Many of the artifacts found there were extremely **fragile**. Sometimes only a pattern of beads was left of a necklace. Some fabrics crumbled into dust when they were touched.

◀ *The rooms in the tomb were piled high with all sorts of valuable objects, including jewelry, furniture, and statues.*

Howard Carter used nearby tomb KV15 as a workshop for cataloging the artifacts from Tut's tomb. There, they were cleaned and photographed before they were moved to a museum in Cairo.

fragile: easily broken or damaged

The Pharaoh's Furniture

Tutankhamun was buried with furniture for his new home in the afterlife. In the tomb were chairs, chests, and four beds. All were beautifully carved with animal heads and decorated with gold. Archaeologists could see that ancient Egypt had very skilled craftsmen.

Leisure in the Afterlife

Those who buried the young pharaoh made sure he would have fun in the afterlife, too. There were several board games in the tomb, as well as many weapons for hunting. There were also six **dismantled** chariots for him to drive in paradise.

◀ *These archaeologists are looking at one of four chariots that were found in the tomb.*

"Details of the room within emerged slowly from the mist, strange animals, statues, and gold—everywhere the glint of gold."

Howard Carter

dismantled: taken apart

The King's Clothes

What can you learn from someone's clothes? Archaeologists could see from the size and shape of the 100 pairs of sandals that Tutankhamun had long, narrow feet. Also in the tomb were 139 canes. They looked like they had been used. This suggested that King Tut had problems walking.

▲ *The sandals found in the tomb were made of wood and decorated with gold and bark. This pair shows enemy prisoners.*

Gold, Silver, and Precious Jewels

In ancient Egypt, pharaohs wore a lot of jewelry. Jewelry was used as both decoration and as protection against evil spirits. Tutankhamun was buried with bracelets, earrings, necklaces, anklets, chains, and rings. These were made of pure gold and silver, **inlaid** with precious stones.

▶ *Pharaohs and wealthy people in ancient Egypt wore a type of jewelry called pectorals. They were often in the form of brooches.*

Egyptian gold came from Nubia (now Sudan) and the desert. Egyptians loved gold because it shone like the Sun and never tarnished, or grew dull. They called it "flesh of the gods."

 inlaid: an item that is set into the surface of another object

Egyptian Art

Artwork and carvings on items in the tomb were like ancient photographs. The images gave archaeologists snapshots into the life of the boy king. Tutankhamun liked to hunt. Paintings show him in his chariot, hunting lions and ostriches, or squatting in the reeds hunting ducks.

▲ *One wall of Tut's tomb was covered with pictures of him being guided by Egyptian gods and goddesses.*

Married Life

Other pictures give us a glimpse into Tut's personal life. His golden throne is decorated with images of him with his wife, Ankhesenamun. She is gently **anointing** him with perfume. Other scenes show her handing him arrows while he hunted. They seemed very fond of each other.

Tutankhamun had no intention of going hungry in the afterlife. There were 40 gallons of wine and meat from geese, ducks, and oxen buried with him!

 anointing: blessing someone, usually with oil or perfume

37

The Antiquities Service

Until the 1800s, artifacts from ancient sites in Egypt were not protected. Jewelry, statues, and even entire monuments could be packed up and shipped to other countries. In 1858, the **Antiquities** Service of Egypt was created. This government department passed laws to keep artifacts in Egypt.

▲ *Touring exhibitions about Tutankhamun and Egypt's other pharaohs are popular all over the world.*

Tut's Treasures on Display

Carnarvon and Carter had to hand over all the items they found. They would go on display in the Cairo Museum. Some people believe that Carter and Carnarvon smuggled some items out for themselves. Certainly, artifacts from the tomb have turned up in other countries.

▶ *The death mask from Tut's tomb is now one of the most famous and popular attractions on display at the Egyptian Museum in Cairo.*

"**All objects from the tomb should be in Egypt, and if they're not in Egypt, they didn't get out legally.**"

Egyptologist Dr. Christian Loeben

 antiquities: objects from ancient times

Revealing Tut's Secrets

The Curse of Tutankhamun

Ancient Egyptians believed that mummies were protected by spirits. A curse would fall on anyone who disturbed a grave or robbed a tomb. The curse might cause illness, bad luck—or even death. The curse was often written on the walls of the tomb as a warning to those who entered.

▲ *Carter (left) and Carnarvon (right) did not believe in ancient Egyptian curses, but Carnarvon died within a few months of opening the tomb.*

Mysterious Deaths

Howard Carter did not believe in curses. He ignored the warnings from local people and opened Tut's tomb. A few months later, Lord Carnarvon died from an infected mosquito bite. By 1929, 11 people from Carter's team had died. One of the victims of the curse was Richard Bethell, Carter's personal secretary. He was found **smothered** to death in his bed.

▲ *This carved curse was found at the entrance to the tomb of a man named Petety. The curse ends with the words: "Anyone who does anything bad to my tomb, then the crocodile, hippopotamus, and lion will eat him."*

"As for any man who shall destroy these, it is the god Thoth who shall destroy him."

Tomb curse

smothered: not allowed to breathe

How Did Tut Die?

The discovery of Tutankhamun's mummy solved some mysteries, but it also created new ones. Scientists wondered what caused his death. Was he murdered? X-rays and special scans showed he had broken his leg in a fall. He also had **malaria**. These two things together may have killed him.

▲ *By studying his preserved body, scientists were able to find out a lot about this pharaoh who had died so young.*

Tut's Family

Modern science was also used to prove who Tut's parents were. DNA testing showed that his father was Akhenaten. His mother was traced to a female mummy found in another tomb. Her name is not known, but she was one of Akhenaten's sisters.

▶ *Advances such as DNA testing finally solved the mysteries of Tutankhamun's family tree. They showed that his father was the famous pharaoh Akhenaten, who worshiped only the Sun.*

It was very common in ancient Egypt for royalty to marry their siblings. They believed this would keep the bloodline pure. Tut's wife, Ankhesenamun, was his half-sister.

 malaria: a disease spread by mosquitoes that causes fever

Tut Today

Some of the artifacts from Tut's tomb have been displayed on tours around the world. Millions of people have gazed upon the treasures of a boy king who lived more than 3,000 years ago. Forgotten for thousands of years, today, he is the most famous Egyptian pharaoh.

New Discoveries

Amazing discoveries are still being made in Egypt. Two new tombs were discovered in 2008 in the Valley of the Kings. One held five mummies but no grave goods. The other is the tomb of a royal court singer. New technologies such as **satellite imagery** may reveal the location of new pyramids, now buried in the sand.

▼ *Workers are still excavating in the Valley of the Kings. Who knows what treasures might still lie beneath the sand and rock?*

The Supreme Council of Antiquities is trying to get back artifacts that were taken from Egypt long ago. Some have already been returned. One of these was a mummy displayed for many years at the Daredevil Hall of Fame in Niagara Falls, Canada. It was proven to be the mummy of the pharaoh Ramses I.

satellite imagery: pictures taken from space

Learning More

Books

Hail! Ancient Egyptians
by Jen Green
(Crabtree Publishing, 2010)

Inside the Tomb of Tutankhamun
by Jacqueline Morley
(Enchanted Lion Books, 2005)

King Tut's Tomb
by Doering Tourville
(Capstone Press, 2008)

Tutankhamun
by Gill Harvey
(Usborne Books, 2006)

Tutankhamun and Other Lost Tombs
by John Malam
(QEB Publishing, 2011)

Tutankhamun: The Mystery of the Boy King
by Zahi Hawass
(National Geographic Children's Books, 2005)

Websites

www.kingtutone.com
Ancient Egypt Online: a website of resources about the world of the pharaohs.

http://ngkids.co.uk/cool_ stories/1410/tutankhamun_ facts_
The National Geographic Kids website about King Tut.

www.historyforkids.org/ learn/egypt/
History for Kids—all about ancient Egypt.

http://eurekids.wordpress. com/2010/02/13/king-tut- videos/
Videos about Tutankhamun.

Glossary

advisors Experts who give advice to a leader

afterlife Life after death

amateur Someone who does something as a hobby not a job.

anointing Blessing someone, usually with oil or perfume

antiquities Objects from ancient times

archaeologist Someone who studies ancient people

canyon A deep valley with steep sides

dismantled Taken apart

fragile Easily broken or damaged

inlaid An item that is set into the surface of another object

intact Not broken or touched in any way

malaria A disease spread by mosquitoes that causes fever

papyrus A type of paper made from the stems of reed plants

preserved Kept in its original condition

rituals Special ceremonies to mark particular events

rubble Pieces of stone left over from a building

sarcophagus A large stone coffin with smaller coffins inside

satellite imagery Pictures taken from space

siblings Brothers and sisters

smothered Not allowed to breathe

tribute A gift made to show respect

Index

Entries in **bold** refer to pictures

afterlife 16, 20, 21, 22, 32, 33
Akhenaten 9, 43, **43**
Amarna 10, **10–11**
Ankhesenamun 37, 43
Antiquities Service of Egypt 38
Aten 9

Bethell, Richard 41
board games 33
bow and arrows 13, **14**
Brier, Bob 21
burial chamber 28, 29

Cairo Museum 31, 39
canes 34
canopic jars 23, **23**
Carnarvon, Lord 4, 5, 6, 7, 27, 28, 39, **40**, 41
Carter, Howard 4, 5, **5**, 7, 26, **26**, 27, 28, **28–29**, 30, 31, 33, 39, **40**, 41
cartouches 11, **11**
chariots 13, **14**, **32**, 33, 36
clothes 10, 21, 34, **34**
curses 40, 41, **41**

death mask 29, **39**
Deir el-Medina **18– 19**, 19

education 11

festivals 14
food 10, 21, 37
furniture 21, 32

gods 9, 14, 20
gold 29, 32, 33, 35

hieroglyphics 11, **11**
hunting 13, 33, 36

jewelry 21, 31, 35, **35**, 38

Loeben, Christian 39
Luxor 18

Maat 14, 15
malaria 42
mastaba 16, 17
mummies 22, **22**, 23, 28, 29, 40, 42, **42**, 43, 45

Nile River 12, **12–13**
Nubians 15

palaces 8, 9, 10, **10–11**
papyrus 11
pharaohs 6, 8, 9, 14–21, 29, 30, 33, 35, 44, 45
prayers 20
priests 9, 22, 23, 24
pyramids **16–17**, 17

Ramses I 45
Ramses II 25
religion 8, 9

sarcophagus **28–29**, 29
servants 15
shrines 29
Supreme Council of Antiquities 45

temples **8**, 9
tomb robbers 17, 18, 19, 40

Valley of the Kings 6, **6–7**, 7, 19, **24**, 25, 26, **44–45**, 45

wall paintings **18**, 20, 36, **36–37**